A Friends Love Story

A Friends Love Story

Tim W. Edwards

Contents

Table of contents

Chapter 1: Between Love and Friendship

In the small, quaint town of Galvin, New Hampshire, 1975, hidden beneath golden leaves and bustling diners lies a story of love, friendship, and discovery. This is the tale of John and Sally, best friends navigating the complexities of their entwined lives. John, thoughtful and sincere, finds solace and joy in his deep bond with Sally. They share everything—laughter over dinners, adventures across state lines, and even moments of intimacy that blur the lines of friendship. Despite the intensity of their connection, a silent storm brews within John. He gradually comes to realize that his feelings for Sally run deeper than camaraderie, blossoming into love. This profound revelation marks the beginning of his internal struggle, as John balances the fear of ruining what they have with the longing for something more. Sally, on the other hand, moves with a carefree spirit. She values her friendship with John, seeing him as her anchor amidst life's uncertainties. Yet, her heart is drawn toward Dylan, a charismatic newcomer in Galvin. Dylan, with his magnetic charm and mysterious past, captures Sally's attention, leaving John to grapple with jealousy and heartache. As these dynamics unfold, the story paints a rich tapestry of the 1970s—a time of change and liberation, set against the backdrop of a close-knit community. Galvin, with its picturesque landscape and town gatherings, becomes a character in itself, shaping the lives of its inhabitants with its timeless rhythms. Central to the narrative are the poignant moments of introspection and confrontation. John's journey is one of courage and vulnerability, as he teeters on the edge of revealing his true feelings to Sally.

The tension between friend and lover forces both characters to confront their fears and desires, leading to pivotal conversations and intense emotional exchanges. The plot crescendos at a town festival—a vibrant celebration under the autumn sky—where secrets unravel and truths come to light. Sally finds herself caught between familiarity and the allure of new love, facing decisions that could alter the course of her future. Themes of unrequited love, friendship, and the pursuit of happiness weave through each chapter. Questions arise about the nature of relationships: Can love truly blossom from friendship? Is it possible to risk losing a friend in the hope of gaining a lover? The story explores these dilemmas with sensitivity and depth. The narrative follows a fluid arc, beginning with lighthearted encounters and deepening into an emotionally charged exploration of love and loyalty. As the story unfolds, the reader is drawn into the lives of John, Sally, and Dylan, experiencing their joys and sorrows firsthand. The climax arrives with an unexpected revelation—one that challenges the characters' perceptions of love and forces them to decide whether to embrace their true feelings or retreat into the safety of the past. This moment not only tests their relationships but also their understanding of self and each other. In its conclusion, "Between Love and Friendship" offers a resolution that is as tender as it is truthful. It reflects on the enduring nature of friendship, the transformative power of love, and the courage required to follow one's heart. A gentle epilogue hints at the characters' future paths, leaving readers with a sense of hope and the reminder that every heartache is a stepping stone to self-discovery.

Chapter 2: Beginnings in Galvin

In the early days of fall, the town of Galvin transformed into a picturesque landscape, with leaves cascading like confetti from ancient maples, painting the streets in shades of amber and crimson. This was the time of year when John and Sally felt most at home. Both natives of Galvin, they had grown up amidst the gentle hum of crickets and the comforting clang of the church bell that echoed through Main Street every Sunday morning. John and Sally had formed a bond as enduring as the river that wound gently through the outskirts of their town. From their earliest memories of skinned knees and tree-climbing adventures, they were two inseparable halves of a whole. Their friendship matured under the watchful eyes of Galvin's close-knit community, where everyone knew each other's stories and secrets. Every Friday evening, without fail, they would find themselves at Max's Diner. Under the warm glow of neon lights and over plates of pecan pie, they spun dreams and shared their lives, trading stories as effortlessly as breathing. John, with his thoughtful brown eyes and reassuring presence, would listen intently, absorbing each word Sally shared. Their friendship was seasoned with familiarity, a rich tapestry woven with shared histories. They had traversed New Hampshire's winding roads together, their travels taking them from the rocky shores of Rye Beach to the rolling forests of White Mountain. With each trip, their laughter left lingering echoes across the landscapes they passed through, solidifying their bond. Such was the nature of their relationship, a symphony of shared moments and mutual understanding. Yet, amidst this symphony, a single note of discord silently grew within John. His feelings for Sally had begun to deepen, trickling into the sacred domain of unspoken desires. Where once he saw a friend, he now saw a woman whose laughter lit up his world, whose mere presence was a promise of contentment. As autumn days waned and nights grew longer, John found himself facing the quiet turmoil of his heart. How could he express these feelings without risking the profound camaraderie they cherished? It was a question that plagued him, woven into the fabric of their interactions like an invisible thread. Sally, ever spirited and full of life, remained blissfully unaware of the silent storm within John. Her eyes were set on new horizons and new faces. Dylan, the intriguing newcomer who had recently settled into Galvin, with his enigmatic smile and effortless charm, captured Sally's curiosity. This budding interest was something she shared openly during their late-night conversations, not realizing the twinge of jealousy it sparked in John. This was the heart of their friendship—one rooted in the soil of their shared past, now facing the winds of change. As John grappled with his feelings, Galvin bore witness to their journey, its autumnal beauty serving as both a backdrop and a participant in their intricate dance. In this small town, bound by tradition and the passage of time, John and Sally stood on the precipice of something transformative. Whether it would lead to clarity or confusion was a question only the unfolding chapters could answer.

Chapter 3: Unseen Emotions

The gentle hum of autumn in Galvin whispered a lullaby of change as John meandered through the town's familiar streets. Each step echoed the rhythm of his internal struggle, a symphony of hidden emotions composed less of notes and more of heartbeats. The leafy paths, trodden countless times with Sally by his side, now seemed tinged with a potent mix of nostalgia and yearning. Their friendship had always been a constant, a sanctuary from the chaos of the world outside. Yet, as the days grew shorter, John found himself examining the unspoken layers of their relationship. Moments once shared with innocent camaraderie now took on a weightier significance. Each touch, each smile exchanged over dinner at Max's Diner, felt charged with an unacknowledged energy. John knew Sally noticed none of this silent transformation. In her laughter and light-hearted chatter, she embodied a freedom he both envied and cherished. It was during these moments, when Sally's gaze flicked over him without really seeing, that John grappled with his growing realization. His simple affection for her had matured into something dangerously akin to love. A love he dared not confess. Their intimate moments, the ones that crossed the comfortable boundary of friendship into something more physical, had started as mutual, uncomplicated curiosity. Neither of them sought labels or complications; it was merely a testament to their trust and connection. But for John, each encounter became a testament to the depth of his feelings—longing seeping steadily into the spaces between laughter and soft touches. Yet, fear anchored him. He feared the truth of his heart more than the silence in which it thrived. Confessing could mean changing everything—potentially losing the ease and safety they shared. And so, he kept his emotions muted, a landscape of unseen love, rich yet deliberately unexplored. Meanwhile, Sally remained blissfully indifferent to the turmoil within John. Her interest had shifted, fueled by the presence of Dylan. Dylan, the new enigma in Galvin, had a way of capturing attention, not through overt charm, but through his quiet confidence and intriguing backstory. Sally, with her curious nature, was drawn to him, while John could only watch, his heart hitching with unvoiced agony. In those moments where Sally spoke of Dylan, her eyes lit with intrigue and possibility, John found it hard to maintain his usual easy smile. He perfected the art of listening without revealing his inner disquiet, a talent he wished he didn't have to possess. As the autumn days lingered on, John found solace in the rituals of their friendship. An evening drive along the river, their laughter interwoven with the rustling of leaves, became both a balm and a reminder of what could never be spoken. Yet, as inevitable as the changing seasons, his love for Sally persisted, silently insistent. Galvin observed this unspoken journey, its landscapes cradled in the whispers of unseen emotions. In the rustle of leaves and the cadence of life's cycles, John's heartbeats kept time, marching silently alongside the evolving autumn rhythm—a melody of longing and restraint amongst the rustic charm of their familiar, beloved town.

Chapter 4: Whispers of Change

The crisp New Hampshire air was tinged with anticipation, a promise of change lingering in the rustling of the autumn leaves. For John, walking through the familiar streets of Galvin, each step felt heavier under the weight of unspoken truths. The town itself seemed to sense the subtle shifts—its quaint charm holding space for the silent dramas that unfolded in the lives of its residents. John's routine walks, usually a source of solace, had turned into solitary journeys steeped in contemplation. He found himself gravitating toward the willow-lined banks of the river, where the world felt still, listening as if waiting for him to find the words he couldn't speak. This was the place where he let his mask slip, where he could face the truth that his heart was no longer his own. Despite his intentions to keep his feelings hidden, the shadows of longing crept into his every interaction with Sally. They shared their evenings as they always had, his presence at her side a constant comfort. Yet, each laugh and shared glance felt to John like lines blurred, soft reminders of what he yearned for but feared to claim. On an October night under a blanket of stars, Sally and John lay side by side on the grassy hill overlooking Galvin. The town stretched below them, a patchwork of warm lights and quiet lives. Sally pointed out constellations, her voice animated, oblivious to the storm swirling within John. "Look, that one's Orion," she said, tracing the outline with her fingertip against the sky. John followed her gesture, his heart heavy with the weight of unuttered words. "Yeah, I see it," he replied softly, his gaze slipping from the stars to her profile. In the faint glow of moonlight, he saw everything that tied him to her and everything that held him back—a friendship so dear it defied easy explanation, a bond tested but never broken. Sally's fascination with Dylan added another layer to his turmoil. She spoke of him often, her curiosity evident in every word. Dylan was a figure of mystery and allure, something new and exciting. While Sally's intrigue was natural, it was a thorn in John's heart, a reminder of possibilities he couldn't offer. "She mentioned going to that new art exhibition with him,"John recalled her telling him the other day, her excitement palpable. He had nodded, maintaining the facade of encouragement expected of a friend, but inside his insecurities festered. His mind wandered to those moments with Sally, when the line between friendship and something more had been momentarily eclipsed. Those encounters, tender yet undefined, felt like echoes of what could be—a dance on the precipice of deeper connection, stirring the shadowy longings within him. As he lay beside Sally, contentment battled with his unshed confessions. He longed to reach out, to break the spell of silence and share the truth of his heart. Yet, paradoxically, it was this very closeness he feared losing—a connection too precious to risk, his deeper feelings locked away in a silent chamber of his soul. For now, the shadows of longing whispered only to John, their echoes woven into the tapestry of an autumn that seemed uniquely his. The town of Galvin continued to hold its breath, waiting patiently as time folded into itself, carrying John's secret forward with the inevitability of change.

Chapter 5: A New Arrival

The arrival of Dylan in Galvin was like a gust of wind sweeping through the town, stirring interest and whispers among its residents. Dylan was the kind of newcomer that captured attention without trying, his presence infused with a quiet intensity that made people pause and take notice. His past was a tapestry of intriguing stories left untold, and this air of mystery was precisely what drew Sally to him. Dylan set up shop in a modest cabin just beyond the edge of town, nestled among tall pines that stood as sentinels of time. His arrival had been unexpected yet warmly welcomed, as is the custom in Galvin to embrace new faces with open curiosity rather than suspicion. The town's grapevine buzzed with speculative chatter about who he was and why he'd chosen their quaint town as his new abode. Sally was instantly captivated. Her affection for new experiences and expanding horizons found a beacon in Dylan. He was the otherworldly excitement she had yearned for, a way to step beyond the familiarity that her life in Galvin had always held. When she first met him at a community event — a pumpkin festival alive with laughter and autumn cheer — Sally was struck not just by his charisma, but by the life stories that seemed to linger in his gaze. Their conversations unfolded easily, like pages turning in a book. Dylan spoke of his travels, the places he'd called home, and the myriad adventures that had brought him to Galvin. Each tale was a piece of his patchwork past, wrapped in intrigue and softened by the gentle accent of distant places. To Sally, he offered a world of unexplored possibilities, a universe far removed from her roots with John. As Sally's interest in Dylan grew, John struggled to mask the inner conflict this sparked. While Sally recounted her latest interaction with Dylan, her eyes sparkling with enthusiasm, John felt an uninvited knot of jealousy tighten within him. He silently observed the subtle shifts in her attention—a gaze that once found him across rooms now wandered to where Dylan stood. Dylan had a presence that was undeniable, and John was acutely aware of how Sally's gaze lingered a moment too long or how her laughter took on a different note when she spoke of Dylan. John tried to maintain an easy demeanor, all the while feeling the balance of their trio teeter precariously. Unbeknownst to Sally, the arrival of Dylan had served not only as a catalyst for her curiosity but also as a pivotal point in John's silent battle. John wrestled with the realization that Dylan might reflect something he couldn't—a world beyond the comfortable boundaries of Galvin, one filled with the potential of new and exciting paths. Galvin, with its languid river and endless fields batting against time, had borne witness to these new stirrings brought by Dylan. The town watched quietly, its role as a nurturing backdrop constant and unchanged even as human dynamics unfolded within its embrace. As autumn leaves clung stubbornly to their branches, John faced the growing struggle of holding onto what he had with Sally, even as she seemed to shift her attention to the possibilities Dylan represented. The irony was not lost on him that the change he feared was as inevitable as the turning of the seasons, and yet, it was a change he was powerless to avert. In this new phase, their friendship was entering uncharted territory, with the landscape of their lives shaped forever by the arrival of one man who unknowingly held the power to shift the dynamics of an enduring friendship entrenched in mutual affection and untold truths

Chapter 6: Crossing the Line

The first chill of November settled over Galvin like a gossamer veil, coaxing the townsfolk indoors to the warm embrace of hearths and friendships. For John and Sally, it was a season of reflection, their routines as familiar as the yellowing photograph pinned inside the arm of John's favorite jacket. The bond they shared was deepening, taking on colors richer than the autumn leaves that painted their path. On a particularly crisp evening, John and Sally found themselves ensconced in the cozy corners of Sally's living room. The flicker of a single candle cast whimsical shadows across the walls, their faint movements a backdrop to the melody of crackling logs in the fireplace. "Do you remember the trip we took to Boston?" Sally asked, her voice soft with the wistfulness of remembrance. They were sprawled on the carpet, a haphazard picnic of cheese and apples laid between them. Sally's eyes reflected the firelight, lending them an adventurous glint that John found irresistibly endearing. John chuckled, retrieving the memory like a favorite book. "How could I forget? You nearly dragged us into every bookstore in the city." It was in these moments—these pockets of cherished time—that John felt the fusion of their souls. Conversation flowed between them like an unending stream, connecting the past, the present, and an uncertain future with unspoken promises. As the evening unfolded, laughter subsided into a comfortable silence. The kind where words became superfluous, leaving space for the heart to absorb what the lips could not express. Sally's head found its place on John's shoulder, and the innocent weight of her presence ignited a desire deeper than friendship—a yearning that clung to the edge of his consciousness. Their physical relationship, once a shared exploration of curiosity, had quietly evolved into an extension of their emotional bond. It was a line crossed, a step taken into a territory without maps or clear direction. John frequently found himself lingering in this space, reveling in the softness of Sally's laughter, in the way her hand fit perfectly in his. Tonight, as his mind danced on the precipice, John felt the familiar urge to speak. The words he longed to say hovered like birds poised in silent flight. But each time, he hesitated, fearing that voicing his love would scatter their perfect companionship to the winds of what might never be. Instead, he turned lightly to rest his chin atop her head, drawing comfort from the tangible proof of their connection. In those intangible moments of closeness, everything was distilled to pure simplicity. No titles or definitions could cage what they felt, yet it was both more and less than the love songs adored by the world. Sally stirred beside him, breaking the spell. "Do you think we'll always be like this, John? Just us, against the world?" Her question hung in the air, filled with an innocence and naivety that tugged at his heart. "I hope so," he replied, the sincerity in his voice a fragile echo of his desires. Hope was all he could offer—hope that this balance they shared would not tip into the chaos of unreciprocated love. At moments like this, Dylan's presence loomed at the edges of their shared intimacy, an uninvited guest in the thoughts they never vocalized. Sally's burgeoning interest in Dylan cast a subtle shadow, stretching across the warmth they tried to preserve. Yet for now, in the glow of the firelight and the soothing cadence of Sally's breathing beside him, John allowed himself the luxury of this illusion—a momentary suspension of reality where they existed beyond the bounds of friendship and aspiration. A fleeting space where possibilities danced in the gentle flames, flickering and fragile, as ephemeral as the twilight of a late autumn day.

Chapter 7: An Outsider's Charm

The vibrant hues of autumn in Galvin were slowly surrendering to the grays of a New Hampshire winter, casting a reflective mood over the town's daily life. It was within this shifting scenery that Dylan's presence began to unravel the delicate balance John had fought so steadfastly to maintain. While John remained a steadfast constant, Dylan was an intriguing variable, introducing a ripple of excitement that Sally couldn't help but gravitate toward. Dylan's charm was an unhurried and effortless thing, woven into the very fabric of his being. He carried the air of a man who had seen the world beyond Galvin's borders, his stories painting pictures of exotic landscapes and distant shores. His presence seemed to draw people to him, much like a moth to a flame, Sally included. John watched from the sidelines, his heart a battlefield of conflicting emotions. His bond with Sally, once unchallenged, now felt fragile, as if hanging by a thread above an abyss of unspoken desires and suppressed confessions. He was caught in a delicate dance, aware that one misstep could unravel everything he held dear. For Sally, Dylan represented a world unexplored, a tantalizing promise of new beginnings. She found herself drawn into conversations with him that lasted for hours, discussing everything from music and art to philosophies that felt refreshingly new. They shared a night at a local jazz club, where the rhythmic beats resonated deep within, contrasting sharply with the steady, familiar drum of her friendship with John. It was during one of these encounters, at a town gathering, that John felt Dylan's outsider charm truly take root. The community center was alive with laughter and the warmth of lifelong friends gathered to evade the encroaching chill of winter. Sally stood beside Dylan, her laughter bright and clear against the backdrop of fervent discussions and jovial camaraderie. From across the room, John felt the pang of his heart's silent protest. Dylan effortlessly commanded the attention of everyone around him, Sally's gaze never straying far from his animated face. The ease with which she engaged in their shared conversation was a subtle reminder to John of the wall slowly growing between her world and his. As the evening wore on, John found himself outside, leaning against the cold metal of a nearby streetlamp. The air was biting, yet it felt distant compared to the chill that had settled in his chest. He watched the warm glow of activity spill through the community center's windows, each frame a snapshot of lives continuing, seemingly unfazed by his internal unrest. It was there that Dylan found him. In typical fashion, Dylan's approach carried none of the awkwardness that John might have expected. There was only the quiet understanding of a man who had seen enough of life to recognize the signs of an internal battle. "Quiet out here," Dylan said simply, his voice cutting through the night's silence. John nodded, the words he wanted to say tangled in his throat. There was a beat of silence, one that stretched with the weight of unsaid confessions. "Galvin's been good to me," Dylan continued, a soft smile following his words, "It's a real community. But Sally's something else, isn't she?" John caught the flicker of admiration in Dylan's eyes and felt a twist of anxiety, yet something else entirely—a reluctant recognition of Dylan's genuine interest. It was both a validation of Sally's undeniable allure and a threat to the quiet equilibrium John had cherished. "She's... yeah," John replied, his voice betraying only a fraction of the turmoil inside. "She is." Dylan nodded, perhaps sensing the unvoiced sentiment beneath John's simple agreement. The silence that followed was not tense but shared, as though both men were participants in an unspoken understanding, a mutual respect for the path each tread. In the heart of Galvin, John's world continued to shift, the outsider's charm promising change. Dylan brought with him the fresh air of adventure, a breeze that threatened to carry Sally toward new possibilities. Yet in every trial, there was a lesson to be learned—a truth waiting to be discovered amid the complexities of the heart. As the night deepened, John found himself at the edge of an inevitable decision. To protect what had been or to embrace what could be meant crossing lines both profound and personal. As his resolve strengthened under the unwavering gaze of the stars above, so too did his readiness to face whatever tomorrow might bring. In those silent moments beneath the watchful sky, the journey of John's heart took another step forward into the unknown.

Chapter 8: Internal Conflicts

In the heart of Galvin, as winter's breath whispered through bare branches, John faced a tempest unlike any he had known before—one that resided entirely within. The silent struggle between his heart's desires and his mind's restraint was an all-consuming presence, unfurling like winter fog over the familiar landscape of his soul. John had always been steadfast, an anchor in the lives of those around him, but Sally had become the core of his existence. Their shared history, expanded by trips and tales and tender touches, had blurred into something more profound yet undefined. His love for her, once a whisper, was now a resounding anthem that played incessantly in his thoughts. Each day with Sally was both a blessing and a torment. The simplicity of their friendship—crafted over years of knowing and being known—now seemed a fragile facade against the storm of his feelings. He watched her animated joy as she recounted her latest encounter with Dylan, each mention a soft dagger. Dylan was everything John feared he was not—new, exciting, and drawing Sally toward unfamiliar horizons. The echoes of this internal conflict colored John's world. At work, the numbers he once handled with ease now danced chaotically, reflecting the turmoil in his head. The sight of the town's river, a place of solace and reflection, mirrored his struggle, a constant flow he couldn't contain. In the quiet solitude of his evenings, John often found himself replaying moments he shared with Sally. A look, a lingering touch, or a shared joke—each was dissected and examined from every angle. He longed for the courage to voice his feelings, to risk everything for the chance of something more. Yet, fear of losing Sally, of shattering the delicate tapestry of their lives as they were, kept him silent. Their latest adventure—a spontaneous drive through the snow-dusted lanes leading out of Galvin—provided no answers. Sally's laughter, ringing freely in the confines of the car, contrasted with the quiet battles raging within John. Her voice was the melody of his life, yet the harmony he sought seemed ever elusive. It was late one evening, beneath the cocoon of stars, that John found himself alone on the porch of the cabin Sally and he often retreated to. The night was cold, biting, much like the reality he wrestled with. His breaths hung in the air, each exhale a whisper of restraint. Sally, lost in the comforts of the cabin, unaware, had no clue of his turmoil. She was light incarnate, a burst of warmth in the winter night, oblivious to the shadows lingering in his smile. It was in this solitude that John finally acknowledged the crux of his struggle: his heart had outgrown the friendship that had been its foundation for so long. Yet, the fear of revealing this truth and the potential of shattering their connection kept him ensnared. With the stars as silent witnesses, John resolved to face this storm within. Silence would no longer suffice; it was time to embrace the uncertainty of tomorrow. To find a path where his truth could coexist with his deepest fear, this silent struggle was becoming too much to bear alone. In the quiet of a small town wrapped in winter's embrace, a decision formed. John would no longer keep the truth caged, even if it meant stepping into unknown lands where friendship and love danced precariously. For under the same sky, tethered by unseen bonds, he knew a deeper revelation awaited—a future where secrets unveiled could lead to either heartbreak or a new beginning.

Chapter 9: Torn Attachments

As winter tightened its grip on Galvin, life in the small New Hampshire town continued to move at its measured pace, even as the emotional landscape inside John roiled with unrelenting turbulence. The juxtaposition between the serene external world and his chaotic inner turmoil was a constant reminder of the rift between reality and desire. John found himself increasingly isolated within his own thoughts, the weight of his unspoken love for Sally growing heavier with each passing day. Their friendship, once a sanctuary, now felt like a bittersweet tether—as comforting as it was constraining. Every moment they shared seemed tinged with an invisible thread of unacknowledged tension. Sally, meanwhile, continued to navigate her blossoming interest in Dylan. She was charmed by his worldliness and the stories of his travels that spun a tapestry of new possibilities. Unaware of the depth of John's turmoil, Sally remained her effervescent self, splitting her time between her closest friend and her newfound curiosity. The tear in their attachment unfolded quietly during a brisk December afternoon. John and Sally had taken to the woods surrounding Galvin, their breath frosting in the crisp air as they walked a familiar trail. The silence between them was comfortable, yet John felt it as both a companion and an accuser. Their footsteps crunched over fallen leaves, forgotten remnants of a bygone autumn. Sally's voice broke the quiet, drawing John out of his introspection. "Dylan has invited me to a New Year's Eve gathering at his place. What do you think?" The question, innocent and laden with hope, twisted through John like a gust of icy wind. Here was the manifestation of his deepest fear: Sally moving closer to Dylan, stepping toward a future that might exclude him. John forced a smile, fighting to keep his tone light. "I think it's great, Sal. You should go." The encouragement in his voice belied the pang in his heart, a melody of support that clashed with his desire to keep her close, to prevent the inevitable drift. The torn attachments were no longer shadows; they were the raw edges of a reality he couldn't ignore. Sally searched his gaze for a moment, as if sensing the dissonance in his words. Yet, she found only John's steadfast smile, the mask he wore perfectly attuned to their friendship's rhythm. "Why don't you come too?" she asked, breaking into a playful grin. "It'll be fun!" "I'll think about it," John replied, noncommittal, knowing full well that accompanying them would only deepen the chasm he felt growing between their realities. The invitation was as tempting as it was tormenting—a chance to be part of her world, even if on borrowed time. As the afternoon waned and the shadows lengthened, John returned home grappling with his predicament. He knew something had to change. The unspoken truth of his love hung precariously between them, a secret waiting for resolution. Whatever decision he made, John realized it was time to claim his own stake in their shared story. Yet, the fear of severing the ties that bound them held him in place, a prisoner to his own emotional landscape. In the quiet confines of his room, John picked up his guitar, strumming absentmindedly. Music had always been his refuge, translating the inarticulate whispers of his soul into something palpable. The melody that emerged was a sonnet of longing, of everything he wished he could convey. As 1975 drew to a close, John faced the precipice of a new year poised for change. Galvin remained the same picturesque town, but within its bounds, the tides of personal upheaval were demanding their due. What lay ahead was unclear, but one truth shone brighter than any New Year's Eve light—torn attachments could not forever fetter the heart's desires. John knew that the time was fast approaching when he would have to find the words to bridge the chasm, to confront the intricacies of love, friendship, and the path he hoped might include both.

Chapter 10: Revelations at the Festival

The air was electric with anticipation as Galvin prepared for its annual autumn festival, one of the most cherished events marking the year's waning days. Strung across the town square, vibrant rows of strings gleamed, casting a warm glow that spilled over booths offering homemade pies and cider. The subtle chill in the evening breeze added to the festival's enchanting allure, wrapping cozy shawls around bustling attendees. John stood at the heart of this celebration, surrounded by neighbors whose laughter rose into the night sky. The festival brought with it a sense of continuity, a celebration of life's simple pleasures and the comfort of community—a sentiment that felt temporarily adrift in John's heart amidst his personal uncertainty. He watched as Sally, resplendent in the lighthearted festivity of the evening, moved through the stalls with ease and grace. Her laughter was a melody, weaving through the night and reaching him where he stood, yet the distance between them felt more poignant than ever. Tonight was a celebration not only of season's change but of deeper truths waiting to be revealed, truths he felt apprehensive yet compelled to expose. Amidst the sea of familiar faces, it was Dylan who stood out, an enigmatic figure walking through the throng with Sally by his side. His presence was magnetic, drawing Sally's gaze, her laughter brightening as their conversation carried over the festival's ambient noise. John felt a sharp pang, his heart a silent witness to the evolving dynamic between Sally and Dylan. The festival's lights seemed to blur as John wrestled with himself. The pivotal moment he had feared was approaching with the inevitability of dawn after night—the need to express the truth tethered in his heart. The evening's joviality danced around him, yet his mind was a whirlwind of potential confessions and probable consequences. As the night deepened, John found himself weaving through the crowd, seeking clarity amidst the kaleidoscope of festive lights. On the outskirts of the square, where the noise softened to a distant whisper, he found Sally standing alone, momentarily apart from Dylan and absorbed in the sights. The air between them felt laden with unresolved tension and unspoken sentiments. "Sally, can we talk?" John's voice reached her, carrying the weight of everything unsaid. She turned, her expression open and curious, sensing the gravity threading his words. "Of course," she replied, warmth resonating in her gaze despite the whistle of distant laughter. They walked to a quieter part of the park, the festival's glow a gentle backdrop against Sally's attentive silhouette. John halted and drew a deep breath, the chill of the evening air offering a bracing clarity he hoped would carry him through. "I've been thinking a lot," John began, each word bearing the weight of deliberation and restraint. "About us. About everything." Sally watched him with a patient curiosity, her demeanor gentle, inviting him to continue. John hesitated, searching her eyes for the understanding he desperately hoped to find. "In all our years together, I've come to cherish everything we share. But my heart..." The words faltered, a moment of silence stretching thinly between them. Determined, John pressed on. "My heart wants something more." Sally's eyes softened, a reflection of transparency in her silence as she absorbed John's confession. For a brief, heart-stopping moment, John feared losing her, their friendship hanging precariously over this new chasm of honesty. But then she smiled—a mixture of fondness and gentle regret. "John, I didn't know... I didn't realize. I treasure you more than you know. But Dylan... he's something I feel I need to explore." The honesty in her voice was soft yet firm, a clarity that felt both liberating and final. John faced the truth he knew deep down had always been nestled in their shared history. Sally sought new paths, while his heart was intricately bound to what they'd always known. The festive lights at the festival flickered behind them, casting their shadows long against the winter-touched grass. Though unanswered love burned within him, John found a thread of relief in the acceptance of this revelation. Emotions subsided as clarity dawned. Though parted by divergent desires, the connection between John and Sally remained—albeit repaved with newfound understanding. For now, the festival carried on, a comforting consistency against their changing personal landscapes. Thus, amidst the celebration and brilliant illuminations of Galvin's close-knit community, truths were laid bare beneath the sky. John and Sally found themselves at a newfound crossroad—one where friendship and honesty created bridges where love and longing dared not tread.

Chapter 11: Confrontations and Confessions

As the festival continued in full swing, a gentle hum of vitality resonated through the air, punctuated by the lively chatter of Galvin's inhabitants. The night wore on like a familiar melody, with every note and tempo reflecting the heartbeats of this closely knit community. Yet for John and Sally, this festival was more than just a celebration; it was a poignant intersection of unspoken truths and overdue revelations. John stood on the periphery of the gathering, his mind heavy with the confession he had finally brought to light with Sally. Despite the liberation that came with honesty, his heart ached with the knowledge of her feelings for Dylan—a future unwritten but undoubtedly apart from his own desires. Sally, too, felt the weight of recent revelations. Her encounter with John had left her reflective, caught in the echoes of past affections and the burgeoning promise of new ones. As she maneuvered through the familiar faces of festival-goers, her mind sifted through the kaleidoscope of memories and emotions, seeking clarity in the vibrant chaos around her. Dylan appeared beside her again, his presence steady despite the whirlwind of festivities surrounding them. He offered her a warm smile, one that sought to reassure rather than dazzle. "I saw you talking with John," he said softly, not as a question, but as an observation laced with understanding. Sally nodded, her eyes meeting his with sincerity. "Yes, we... we had a bit of a heart-to-heart." Her voice was introspective, a quiet contrast to the bustling energy around them. "John means the world to me. He's been there through everything." Dylan listened intently, his gaze steady and accepting.

"He's a good man, Sally. Someone who truly cares for you." The words lingered between them, a testament to the respectful boundaries Dylan adhered to. He had always regarded the dynamic between Sally and John with quiet integrity, never overstepping the intricate balance that existed long before his arrival. As they spoke, John watched from afar, a silent participant in this unfolding narrative. Despite the ache in his chest, he found a strange comfort in seeing Sally converse so naturally with Dylan. It was a testament to the shifting sands of their relationships, a nod to the inevitability of change and the importance of accepting its passage. Determination solidified within him—a resolve to support Sally's choices, to honor the love born of friendship, even if that love took a form unrecognizable from his deepest hopes. Fear slowly unfurled its grip, replaced by an understanding of what it meant to set free the bonds he had desperately clung to. Encouraged by this clarity, John approached the pair, his steps ceaselessly confident. "Dylan, Sally," he greeted, his smile a blend of courage and camaraderie. "I wanted to... thank you both. For tonight, for being honest." Dylan clasped John's hand in a firm shake, an unspoken bond of respect passing between them. In that moment, John saw not a rival, but another man who valued Sally for the remarkable person she was. "You have my word, John. I'll make sure she has all the happiness she deserves." Sally's eyes shimmered with unshed tears, a mix of gratitude and the sadness of farewells unspoken yet understood. She stepped forward, embracing John with a fierceness that mirrored the strength of their bond. "You are my best friend, John. That will never change, no matter where our paths lead." There it was—the affirmation he had feared and needed all at once. As they stood there, amidst the festive lights that burned with hope and illumination, John felt an acceptance wash over him. He knew then, that love was not just about possession or desire, but about honoring the journey each person must take. As the festival spun on in a dizzying spiral of jubilation, John, Sally, and Dylan stood together, a trio defined not by the past sepulchres of unrequited feelings but by a newfound harmony in understanding and acceptance. In this small town cradled by New Hampshire's serene embrace, where leaves would soon give way to the blanket of winter's slumber, John found peace in the humbling acceptance of love's many forms—the steadfast ties of friendship and the opening doors of possibilities yet seen. Here, amongst the enduring lights of Galvin's cherished festival, hearts were unburdened, secrets were liberated, and, in the glow of meaningful connections, new paths beckoned gently forward.

Chapter 12: The Turning Point

Winter in Galvin had a way of wrapping the town in a reflective hush, where even the most convoluted of life's dilemmas seemed to find some semblance of clarity amid the frosty silence. For John, this seasonal repose was a backdrop to a turning point he had long anticipated yet dreaded. The festival's revelations had signified a crossroads—a point of acceptance and change he could no longer evade. Wrapped in layers against the biting chill, John walked along the familiar path to the river's edge, a path he and Sally often tread. It was here, amidst the stark beauty of snow-draped branches and the river's low murmur, that he sought solace. The decision to confront the undiscovered country of his future, with or without the comfort of the past, weighed heavily on his mind. Having shared his feelings with Sally, John was faced with the aftermath of liberation and loss. Her gentle rejection—an affirmation of her own path and feelings for Dylan—had been a balm of candor, yet it left him untethered, adrift from the anchorage that had been his foundation. Galvin, resplendent in its winter coat, seemed to echo his internal transition. The town's stillness was a canvas for introspection, offering John space to navigate this juncture with renewed perspective. Here, amidst frostbitten pines and whispering winds, he ruminated on what Sally had meant when she said she needed to explore her feelings for Dylan. Satisfaction welled within him at the vulnerability and honesty they had shared, though tinged with a melancholy acceptance. "I need to let go, don't I?" John spoke aloud to the river, his breath crystallizing into the frosty air. The words, though spoken to no one, felt significant—a verbal admission of the uncharted freedom now before him. In the clarity of this turning point, John found a sense of peace he hadn't anticipated. By relinquishing the fantasies and burdens he had long carried—his unrequited love and fear of losing Sally—he realized that this path, though uncertain, promised personal growth and new beginnings. It was an opportunity to define his future without the shadow of what could have been. Sally had always been the light in his life, her presence radiant and her laughter a constant balm. Now, as friends embarking on distinct journeys, John chose to cherish this truth, allowing it to guide rather than weigh him down. He understood that true friendship, like the river's enduring presence, need not diminish despite diverging paths. Turning from the river's edge, John felt a subtle shift within—the inception of hope. He knew the life he would carve out needed to accommodate this new dynamic with Sally and whatever path Dylan might offer her. Yet, amidst these uncertainties, he saw the potential for self-discovery and the pursuit of dreams perhaps long overshadowed. As he walked back to the heart of Galvin, he felt lighter, unencumbered by the chains of withheld emotion. John realized that love, in its various forms, was an evolving journey, and even an unreciprocated one could forge the brightest of futures. The turning point had come and gone not with a tumultuous upheaval but with a quiet resolve. John was ready to step forward, embracing the unknown, emboldened by the lessons of the past and the wisdom they imparted. In nurturing the roots of friendship, John understood he was sowing the seeds of fresh chapters, where possibilities awaited in the gentle embrace of Galvin's quiet winter dusk. Here, he found the courage to embrace the turning point with open arms and an open heart.

Chapter 13: Echoes of the Future

The gentle fall of snow blanketed Galvin in a serene softness, muffling the town's sounds and casting an ethereal glow over its quaint streets. This winter setting encapsulated the quiet transformation that John had experienced, a metamorphosis reflected not only in the frost-rimmed landscapes but also in the new path his heart had charted. In the weeks following the festival's revelations, John embraced a peace that had eluded him, a contentment borne from acceptance and the promise of renewal. With the dawn of each snow-clad morning, he found clarity in the silence, each day an echo of future beginnings he could now envision without the shadow of unrequited love tethering him to the past. Sally had carved out this new space in his life—a friend and confidante, her bond with him strengthened by shared honesty. Though her path diverged toward Dylan, it did so without the specter of regret between them. Instead, they celebrated the essence of their friendship, a durable connection unfettered by the need for undefined titles or clandestine hopes. As winter melded its quiet hand over Galvin, Sally and Dylan's relationship blossomed, naturally unfolding in the quaint confines of this small town. Dylan's charisma and love for life complemented Sally's zest for new experiences. Their laughter was frequent, a melody of happiness that drifted through the townsfolk, sparking more warmth than the season's chill could suppress. John watched their camaraderie grow from a place of genuine joy, the ache of longing replaced by the satisfaction of seeing Sally embrace the love she had sought. Instead of envy, John found himself inspired, determined to carve his own path as brightly as Sally had found hers. Remaining a constant was the river, its frozen surface a testament to both the enduring elements and dynamic changes that the passage of time inevitably brought. Like the solid river beneath sheets of ice, the heartbeat of Galvin pulsed steadily, nurturing individual dreams while holding onto collective memories. Encouraged by new beginnings, John took up painting, a passion ignited by the vivid landscapes of Galvin. Brush in hand, he allowed creativity to fill the spaces once occupied by unresolved feelings. With each stroke, he painted not only the world outside but also the uncharted territories of his inner landscape—a reflection of hopes untethered and futures unwritten. The community felt the ripple effects of this transformation. Friends and neighbors, knowing the intricacies of unspoken stories weaving through Galvin's fabric, embraced John's burgeoning dreams as their own, affirming the collective resolve in the pursuit of joy. When the first buds of spring dared to bloom, a gathering was called—on the very field that had hosted the festival months prior—now transformed under the first kisses of warmth, the echoes of future joys palpable. Friends gathered to celebrate not just the return of spring but the enduring power of connection and renewal. Sally found John amid the crowd, their embrace warm and familiar. "You're painting again," she mentioned with genuine excitement, her eyes alight with pride. "Yes," John replied, a tenderness in his smile. "There's a certain beauty in starting new, isn't it?" Their gaze lingered, both acknowledging this truth. While love had taken them on separate journeys, the threads of friendship intertwined their lives, continuing to create a tapestry rich with shared memories and mutual respect. As the sun set over Galvin, casting long shadows over embracing friends and hopeful futures, John realized that the echoes of the past had paved the way for their present—a collection of moments rooted in understanding and respect, promising a horizon where each step resonated with possibility. In the heart of this small New Hampshire town, new beginnings wove seamlessly into the tapestry of time, illuminating pathways toward futures bright with promise and dreams yet realized. Here, amidst the timeless rhythm of the seasons, love and friendship revealed their true forms—as enduring companions weaving echoes into the future's vast expanse.